SIMONE BILES

by James Buckley Jr.

Consultant: Ellen Labrecque
Former Editor and Writer
Sports Illustrated Kids

BEARPORT
PUBLISHING

New York, New York

D1376882

Credits

Cover, © Henri Szwarc/Sipa USA/AP Images; 4, © Agência Brasil/Wikimedia; 5, © Mark Reis/Colorado Springs Gazette/TNS/Alamy Live News; 7, © Kohjiro Kinno/Getty Images; 8, © Mike Theiler/UPI/Newscom; 9, © Richard Ulerich/Zuma Press/Newscom; 10, © Richard Wareham Fotografie/Alamy Stock Photo; 11, © Melissa J. Perenson/Cal Sport Media/Newscom; 12, © How Hwee Young/EPA/Newscom; 13, © Xiao Yijiu/Xinhua/Alamy Live News; 14, © Agência Brasil/Wikimedia; 15, © Zhukovsky/Dreamstime; 16, © Foto Arena LTDA/Alamy Live News; 17, © PCN Photography/Alamy Stock Photo; 18, © Shopland/BPI/Rex Features via AP Images; 19, © Kyodo via AP Images; 20, © Ron Sachs/dpa/picture-alliance/Newscom; 21, © Matt Dunham/AP Photo; 22T, © Tatyana Zenkovich/EPA/Newscom; 22B, © Goya Artworks/Dreamstime; 23, © Jack Sullivan/Alamy Stock Photo.

Publisher: Kenn Goin
Editor: Jessica Rudolph
Creative Director: Spencer Brinker
Production and Photo Research: Shoreline Publishing Group LLC

Library of Congress Cataloging-in-Publication Data

Names: Buckley, James Jr. author.
Title: Simone Biles / by James Buckley Jr.
Description: New York : Bearport Publishing Company, Inc., 2018. | Series:
    Amazing Americans | Includes bibliographical references and index. |
Identifiers: LCCN 2017012309 (print) | LCCN 2017015918 (ebook) | ISBN
    9781684022953 (ebook) | ISBN 9781684022410 (library)
Subjects: LCSH: Biles, Simone, 1997—Juvenile literature. | Gymnasts—United
    States—Biography—Juvenile literature. | Women gymnasts—United
    States—Biography—Juvenile literature.
Classification: LCC GV460.2.B55 (ebook) | LCC GV460.2.B55 B83 2018 (print) |
    DDC 796.44092 [B] —dc23
LC record available at https://lccn.loc.gov/2017012309

For more information, write to Bearport Publishing Company, Inc., 45 West 21st Street, Suite 3B, New York, New York 10010. Printed in the United States of America.

10 9 8 7 6 5 4 3 2 1

CONTENTS

Dreaming Big

It was the gymnastics finals at the 2016 Olympics. Simone Biles was in the lead to win the **all-around** gold medal. She just needed to nail the **floor exercise**. Would she be able to make her dreams come true?

The 2016 Olympics took place in Rio de Janeiro, Brazil.

The opening ceremony of the 2016 Olympics

Simone does a back handspring during the floor exercise.

A New Goal

Simone Biles was born on March 14, 1997, in Columbus, Ohio. She later moved to Spring, Texas, where she grew up. When Simone was just six years old, she went on a class field trip to a gym. She saw girls flipping in the air and walking across a narrow beam. At that moment, Simone knew she wanted to be a gymnast.

Simone was adopted by her grandparents, Ron and Nellie Biles, when she was six years old.

Simone with Ron and Nellie

Rising Star

Young Simone began taking gymnastics classes. She worked with coach Aimee Boorman. Simone practiced very hard. Soon, she started competing at gymnastics **meets**.

Simone had great power and skill. In 2012, she won the **vault** event at the U.S. National Gymnastics Championships!

Coach Aimee Boorman with Simone

Simone also competed on the balance beam at the 2012 Nationals.

Simone is just 4 feet 8 inches tall (1.4 m).

World Champ!

In 2013, at a U.S. meet, Simone fell off the balance beam—twice. She was so upset that she almost quit gymnastics. After thinking it over, Simone decided to stick with the sport she loved. Later that year, she won the all-around World Championship! Simone was the first African American to earn that title.

Simone holds her gold medal at the 2013 Worlds.

Simone sticks her landing after performing an uneven bars routine.

Women's gymnastics includes four skills: balance beam, floor exercise, vault, and uneven bars.

On to the Olympics

Simone continued to train every day, always with a smile. Her hard work paid off. She won the all-around World Championship again in 2014 and 2015. She was the first woman ever to get three straight world titles. Her huge success helped her earn a spot on the 2016 U.S. Olympic team!

The 2016 U.S. women's gymnastics team included: Aly Raisman, Madison Kocian, Laurie Hernandez, Gabby Douglas, and Simone.

Simone lines up
for a backflip on
the balance beam.

Simone
won four straight
U.S. National
titles, from 2013
to 2016.

13

Champions Together

At the Olympics in Rio, Simone led a powerful U.S. team. They flipped, tumbled, danced—and grabbed the gold medal! Simone helped her team win by earning high scores in three events. She loved competing with her teammates, who were also great friends.

Simone and her teammates wave to fans.

The U.S. team of five gymnasts called themselves the "Final Five."

Simone's high score in the uneven bars helped her team win gold.

The World's Best

Because Simone had done so well, she was in the running for an all-around gold medal. She was up against the best gymnasts in the world.

After a few events, the score was close. It came down to the floor exercise. Simone took a deep breath, and then she ran and leaped high. She spun in the air and stuck her landings. With her big score, she won the all-around gold medal!

Simone with her all-around gold medal

Simone clinched gold with a stunning floor exercise routine.

There's a floor exercise move that's named after Simone. It's a huge flip with a turn.

More Gold

After winning the team and the all-around golds, Simone competed in three more finals. In the vault, her powerful legs helped her reach top speed. Simone bounded off the **springboard** and flew to a near-perfect landing. Gold medal number three!

In the floor exercise, the fans cheered as Simone stuck her final move. She had earned a fourth gold medal!

Coach Aimee and Simone cry tears of joy.

In Simone's third event final, she won a bronze medal on the balance beam.

Simone pushes off of the "horse" during the vault event.

A Young Hero

At the end of the 2016 Olympics, Simone proudly carried the American flag during the closing ceremony. She was happy for her team and her country. She returned home to cheering crowds in Texas. Through it all, Simone always had a huge smile.

Simone met with Michelle Obama and President Barack Obama.

Simone has won 19 Olympic and World Championship medals. That's the most ever won by an American gymnast!

Simone carries the American flag at the closing ceremony.

Timeline

**Here are some key dates
in Simone Biles's life.**

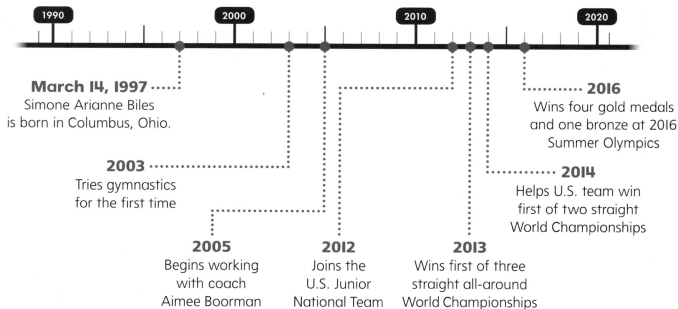

1990   2000   2010   2020

March 14, 1997
Simone Arianne Biles
is born in Columbus, Ohio.

2003
Tries gymnastics
for the first time

2005
Begins working
with coach
Aimee Boorman

2012
Joins the
U.S. Junior
National Team

2013
Wins first of three
straight all-around
World Championships

2014
Helps U.S. team win
first of two straight
World Championships

2016
Wins four gold medals
and one bronze at 2016
Summer Olympics

Glossary

all-around (AWL-uh-round) a gymnastics event that combines scores from four performances

floor exercise (FLORE EX-ur-size) an event in which gymnasts jump, tumble, spin, flip, and dance

meets (MEETS) sports events that usually include individual competitions

springboard (SPRING-bord) a bouncy piece of equipment that helps gymnasts soar high

vault (VAWLT) an event in which a gymnast bounces off a springboard, pushes off a bench, and then soars through the air before landing

Index

Read More

Fishman, Jon. M. *Simone Biles (Sports All-Stars).* Minneapolis, MN: Lerner (2017).

Hansen, Grace. *Simone Biles (Olympic Biographies).* Minneapolis, MN: ABDO (2017).

Learn More Online

To learn more about Simone Biles, visit
www.bearportpublishing.com/AmazingAmericans

About the Author

James Buckley Jr. has written dozens
of books about sports for young readers.

Date: 3/20/18

J BIO BILES
Buckley, James,
Simone Biles /